Looking at the Body

David Suzuki

with BARBARA HEHNER

Stoddart Young Readers

Stoddart

First published in 1987 by
Stoddart Publishing Co. Limited
34 Lesmill Road
Toronto, Canada
M3B 2T6
Second Printing October 1987
Third Printing October 1988
Fourth Printing March 1990

CANADIAN CATALOGUING IN PUBLICATION DATA
Suzuki, David T., 1936-
Looking at the body

ISBN 0-7737-5116-5

1. Body, Human - Juvenile literature. 2. Human physiology - Juvenile literature. I. Hehner, Barbara, 1947- . II. Title.

QP37.S99 1987 j612 C87-093297-7

ILLUSTRATIONS © 1987 Nancy Lou Reynolds
DESIGN: Brant Cowie/Artplus
COVER PHOTOGRAPH: Peter Paterson

Printed in Canada

Table of Contents

AN IMPORTANT NOTE FOR KIDS AND GROWNUPS
You will see this (✋) warning sign on some of the **Things to Do** in this book. It means that an adult should help out. The project may use some boiling water or something might need to be cut with a knife. Everyone needs to be extra careful. Most grownups will want to get involved in these projects anyway—why should kids have all the fun?

Introduction

*H*as your family ever bought a car or house or boat? Remember how carefully all of you looked everything over? After a while, though, you probably started taking your car or house or boat for granted! Well, that's the way it often is with our bodies.

When you skip or catch a ball, shiver in the winter or sweat on a summer day, your body is doing all kinds of complicated things. Most of the time, you're not even aware of it.

Every time I accidentally cut myself and watch my blood harden and the wound slowly heal over, I'm amazed. My digestive system turns cereal, toast, and juice into energy for my muscles to use — and I don't even have to give it a thought. A child's baby teeth come loose one by one, as if they "know" when to make way for permanent teeth.

Some people talk about the body as if it's a machine. They think of the heart as a pump, the bones as a framework, the eye as a camera, the brain as a computer, and so on. It's a simple way of thinking about our bodies, but we mustn't forget that they are far more complex than any machine.

Let's see what we can learn about the many parts and organs that add up to such a wonderful result — your amazing body!

DAVID SUZUKI

Looking at You

*I*n the whole history of the world, there has only been—there will only ever be—one *you*. Even if you have a twin brother or sister who looks just like you, he or she is still a little different. For instance, twins don't have exactly the same patterns of skin on their fingertips.

Each person is different from every other one. Look around as you walk down the street or sit on a bus. People can be tall or short, fat or thin, or anywhere in between. Their hair and skin can be many different colors. They may have curly hair, straight hair, or almost no hair at all. Not only are you different from everybody else—you're also changing all the time. Look at the family photo album. Is that *really* you in the playpen? Look back farther. There's your mother as a teenager. There's your grandfather before his hair turned gray. How you've all changed!

Yet, while human beings are different from each other, there are many ways in which we're all the same. For instance, each of us has a heart to keep blood pumping, lungs to breathe air, a brain to control things, a digestive system to take in food. And all our bodies are made out of cells. Cells are the basic building blocks of living things.

Have you ever seen an *amoeba* under a microscope, or maybe on a TV science show? An amoeba is a tiny living creature that is just one cell. It eats by stretching part of itself out and surrounding a bit of food. The amoeba makes more amoebas by dividing itself in two.

Human bodies are made out of cells, too—about 75,000,000,000,000 (75 trillion) of them. Like the amoeba, these cells can be seen only under a microscope. Some of them—the white blood cells that cruise in our blood gobbling up bacteria—even look quite a bit like the simple amoeba. But human bodies have many different kinds of cells. For instance, muscles cells are long and thin. Red blood cells look like little round saucers. Nerve cells, which carry messages through our bodies, are spidery looking.

Cells group together to make *tissues*. For example, muscle cells are gathered in bundles to form muscle tissue. Body organs are groups of tissues working together on some job your body needs done. Your lungs, heart, liver, and brain are all organs—and there are many others.

Organs, in turn, work together in body *systems*. For example, your mouth, esophagus, stomach, intestines, and other body parts break down food so that your body can use it. They form your digestive system. There are lots of other body systems. Here are just a few of them: The respiratory system specializes in breathing. The excretory system gets rid of wastes. The skeletal system holds you up. Your body, in fact, is an amazing example of co-operation (working together), with each body part doing the right task at the right time.

The Inside Story

Put it together and what have you got? The inside story on you!

What You Need:

a sheet of paper big enough for you to lie on (if you can't find this in an art
    store, tape some smaller sheets together)
colored marker pens
construction paper
scissors
red and blue yarn
white glue
leotard or shorts and T-shirt
reference books and pictures
    about the body
a friend to work with

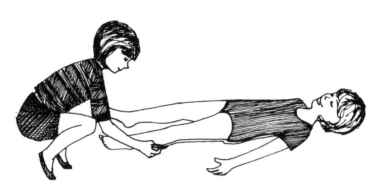

What to Do:

1. Visit the library and find books with drawings of body parts. The librarian can help you. (You can also use the drawings in this book.)

2. Before you make your body drawing, put on a leotard or shorts and a T-shirt. (If you wear bulkier clothes, your friend can't make a good outline of your body.) Lie on your back on the piece of paper. Hold your arms a little out from your sides.

3. Ask your friend to trace all around you. Then you'll have a life-size outline of your body.

4. Now, with construction paper, make some body parts that you can put on your body outline. You might like to include some important organs: brain, lungs, heart, stomach, liver, large and small intestines. You could also include some bones: collarbone, ribs, vertebrae (backbone), pelvis, arm, hand, foot, and leg bones.

5. If you can find a good drawing to guide you, you can also show some of your main blood vessels. Use blue yarn for veins and red yarn for arteries. Draw them on with pencil first. Put a thin line of glue along the pencil lines. Then stick the yarn down.

6. Here are some problems to solve as you do this activity: Where do the body parts go on the outline? How big should they be? It's pretty easy to feel your bigger bones. That tells you where they should go on your drawing. You can also measure them with a string or a tape measure, and cut paper bones the same size.

Organs can be trickier. Try to find drawings that show where they go. Read the text to see if it says about how big the organs are. For instance, your heart is about the size of your clenched fist.

Try to make as good a picture as you can, but don't worry about making some mistakes. You're bound to learn a lot more of your "inside story" than you knew when you began.

Keeping in Touch

How many ways can you make two of your body parts touch each other? This is a good way to exercise and to find out how many different ways you can stretch, bend, and twist.

Let's start with some easy moves:

1. Thumb touch thumb.
2. Nose touch wrist.
3. Finger touch nose.
4. Knee touch elbow.
5. Ear touch shoulder.

Harder:

1. Forehead touch knee.
2. Sole of foot touch sole of foot.
3. Hand touch shoulder blade (shoulder bone in your back).

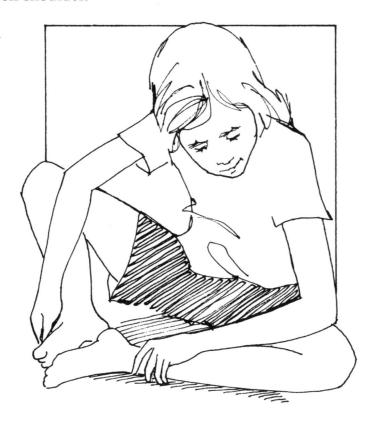

There are hundreds of different combinations. You could make this into a game with a friend. Your friend calls out move, and you try to do it. Every time you do move, you get a point. What keeps your friend from calling out impossible moves—like lips to elbow or tongue to ear? If you try a move and can't do it, you and your friend trade places. The first move your friend has to try is the last one he or she called out. If your friend can't do it, you get 2 points. If your friend *can* do it, though, your friend gets the 2 points.

AMAZING FACTS

Lifespans

What's the longest any human being ever lived? Perhaps it was a man who died in Japan in 1986 at the age of 120. Other people have claimed to be older. However, they didn't have any proof, such as a birth certificate. This man did. It is very rare, though, for someone to live more than 100 years.

A baby girl born in North America now can expect to live to be 78. A baby boy can expect to live to 70. (These are *averages*. Some people will live longer lives; some will live shorter ones.) Why is there an 8-year difference between males and females? Some people who study lifespans think that women live healthier, less tense lives. Others think there is something built right into women's bodies that makes them stronger. Nobody knows for sure.

Games for Each and Every Body

Most kids have run races or played tag. Here are some body workout games that are a little more unusual.

I. Tangled Hop and Push

What You Need:
a friend about your size

What to Do:
1. Make a circle on the ground, with a diameter of 1 to 1.5 m (4 to 5 feet). Do you know what the diameter of a circle is? It's a straight line that goes right across the circle, from one side to the other, passing through the center.

2. You and your friend should both stand inside the circle. Both of you reach behind your back and grab your left foot with your right hand. Now reach behind your back with your left hand and grab your right arm. (This sounds a lot harder than it is. Look at the drawing for help.)

3. The idea now is to hop over to the other person and push him or her out of the circle. You can't be too rough about this, or you'll start to fall over.

4. You win if you push the other person out of the circle, without letting go of your foot and arm.

II. The Great Toes and Elbows Race

What You Need:
some friends to race with
someone to start the race (take turns)
old clothes to wear

What to Do:
1. Mark a starting line. Then mark a finish line about 3 m (10 feet) away. Play on grass or soft ground—this hurts too much on pavement. (You *could* try it with elbow pads, if everybody has a pair.)

2. Lie face down with your friends behind the finish line. Put your hands over your ears. Now lift yourself up on your toes and elbows.

3. When the starter shouts: "GO!" race as fast as you can for the finish line. If you rest your body on the ground or fall over, you have to start over.

Six Impossible Tricks

Human bodies are pretty well built—but there are some things they just can't do.

1. Kiss Your Elbow

Well, can you? I can't—and I never met anyone else who could, either. (No cheating, now—I mean the very tip of your elbow, not the inside of your arm.)

2. Gasp!

Breathe in through your nose. (If you have a cold, you may have to quit right now!) Swallow. Easy? Now breathe in through your nose and swallow *at the same time.* (Nobody can do this. It's a way of keeping breathing separate from swallowing food.)

3. Balance Challenge

Stand beside a wall with your right side against it. Press the edge of your right foot against the wall. Now try to lift your left foot without falling over. (It can't be done. To lift your left foot without losing your balance, you'd have to lean right—but the wall keeps you from doing this.)

4. Sticky Fingers

Press your hand flat against a table with the fingers spread a little. Now lift your hand a bit, and tuck your middle finger under, so that its first two sections are also pressing against the table. Keeping all your other fingers pressed against the table, lift your thumb. No problem? One at a time, lift your baby finger and then your forefinger. Last of all, lift your ring finger. Oh-oh! It's stuck to the table!

Another way to do this one is to press the fingertips of your two hands together. Bend the two middle fingers so that their first and second joints are pressed together. Now try to separate the two ring fingers. They seem glued together.

5. Hey, Your Eyes Are Stuck!

Look straight ahead. Now roll your eyeballs up as if you were trying to roll them back in your head. Don't tilt your head back. Close your eyelids. *With your eyes rolled up*, try to open your eyes again. (Your eye muscles won't let you do it.

They're already keeping your eyes rolled up—and they'd have to work in the opposite direction to let you raise your lids.)

6. Wiggle Your Ears

Are you getting tired of trying to do impossible things? Well, this one *isn't* impossible—it's just hard. Everyone has ear-wiggling muscles, but most of us have no idea how to work them. Practice while looking in a mirror.

Useless Bits?

Some body parts don't seem good for much. For instance, there's that little floppy piece of tissue hanging down at the back of your throat. It's called the *uvula*. People who draw cartoons like to show it wobbling when their characters open their mouths to sing or shout. The uvula has no use that anyone knows about.

We have another seemingly useless bit called the *vermiform* (worm-shaped) *appendix*. It's a "dead end" near one end of your large intestine. In some animals, an appendix may help to digest food, but it doesn't seem to help humans. Sometimes it causes a big pain. A person's appendix can get so sore and puffed up that it has to be removed by a doctor. And the person never misses it.

Body Mysteries

We still have no answers to many of the biggest questions about our bodies.

- Why do we sleep? We spend about a third of our lives sleeping. We feel awful when we don't get enough sleep. So far, though, we're not sure why our bodies need sleep.
- Why do we dream? Is a dream just an accident, a side-effect while our brains are doing something else? Or does it help us solve our problems? No one knows for sure.
- Why do we age? Why do our bodies wear out and die? We know that aging is built right into our body cells. Every day, millions of our cells die and are replaced. The older we get, though, the more slowly cells are replaced. But why does this happen? We don't know — yet.

Your Skin

Suppose that on your birthday somebody gave you an amazing space-age suit. When you were cold, it would warm you up. When you were hot, it would cool you down. No matter how much rain fell, the suit would always keep you dry. It could keep out germs, and cushion you if you fell. And if it ripped, the suit would repair itself!

You already have a suit like this. Some people call it your birthday suit, because it's what you were wearing when you were born. It's your skin. Your skin suit is only a couple of millimetres (one-hundredths of an inch) thick. The thinnest skin is in your eyelids. The thickest, toughest skin (about 5 mm or $\frac{1}{5}$ inch thick) is on the soles of your feet.

Your skin is just loose enough to let you move around. If you stretch out your fingers, you can see little wrinkles on your knuckles. When you make a fist, the knuckle skin smooths out to let your fingers bend. Not only does your skin stretch when it needs to, but it also snaps right back into place. Try pinching up some skin on your arm. As soon as you let go, your arm looks smooth again.

The outer layer of your skin is called the *epidermis*. Every time you wash your hands or dry yourself with a towel, some of your epidermis flakes off. This is nothing to worry about. It's always being replaced by new skin growing up from underneath. The epidermis makes a waterproof coat for your body. It also keeps bacteria and viruses from getting inside you and making you sick.

Epidermis cells have a lot of a tough protein called *keratin* in them. Your nails are also made out of keratin. The part of your fingernail that you can see is dead—that's why it doesn't hurt to clip your nails. The living part is under the skin at the base of the nail. Fingernails are handy for scratching itches and picking up small things. But their main use is to protect your fingertips, which are full of nerve endings and easily hurt.

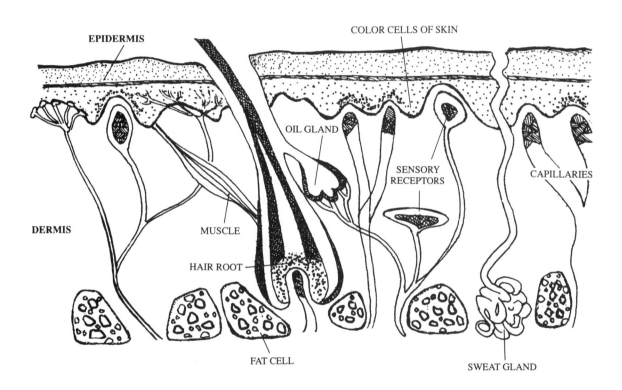

Under the epidermis is a thicker layer of skin called the *dermis*. If you've ever thought of your skin as just a bag that holds you together, think again. The dermis is full of important things, including your body's cooling/heating system. The dermis is threaded with tiny blood vessels called *capillaries*. When you are getting too hot, these blood vessels open wider so that more blood can flow through them. As the blood flows, heat leaves your body through your skin.

The dermis also has sweat glands in it—about 100 for every square centimetre of your skin (or about 650 for every square inch). Sweat is a salty liquid that seeps out of little holes in your skin called *pores*. As it evaporates (turns into gas), it cools you down.

When you're getting too cold, the blood vessels in your skin constrict (get smaller). This helps you save your body heat. A layer of fat just below your dermis also holds in heat. This fat gives your body a smooth, rounded shape. It also protects your bones and organs from bumps and jolts.

There are hair roots in your dermis, too. The roots are the living part of your hair. The part of your hair that you can see is dead keratin, like fingernails. That's why a haircut doesn't hurt—but having your hair tugged out by the roots does. You have hair all over your body, except for the soles of your feet and the palms of your hands. (Your soles and palms have a special "non-skid" surface that's covered with ridges.) Most of your body hair is fine and short. Only the hair on your head grows long. Beside each hair root is an oil gland. The oil keeps your hair from getting too brittle, and it also keeps your skin soft.

Your dermis has many special nerve endings called *sense receptors*. These send sense messages to your brain. Your skin can tell wet from dry, hot from cold, and smooth from rough. Pain receptors in your skin warn you that you've cut yourself. Pressure receptors can feel a tiny insect walking up your arm. Your skin keeps you in touch with the world in many ways.

Why do some of us have dark skin, and some have lighter-colored skin? There is a pigment (coloring chemical) in our skin cells called *melanin*. If we have a lot of it, our skin is brown or black. If we don't have much, our skin is lighter colored. In light-skinned people, more melanin forms when they are out in the sun. We call this a suntan. If the melanin gathers in little patches, it makes freckles.

The blood flowing through our skin also colors it. This pinkish color can be seen more easily in lighter-skinned people, especially in lips, which have many blood vessels and very thin skin.

One human heart is much like another. So are human lungs and livers and muscles. Actually, the main way we look different from each other goes no deeper than our few millimetres of skin!

Soap on a Rope

Old soap scraps can be recycled into a great gift—or a handy item for your own bathtub scrubs.

What You Need:
a cupful of soap scraps
a piece of *soft* cord (remember, it's going to be around someone's bare
    neck) about 40 cm (16 inches) long
a double boiler
a stirring spoon
styrofoam coffee cup
food coloring in your favorite color

What to Do:

1. Pour some tap water into the bottom of the double boiler.

2. Put the soap scraps into the top of the double boiler. Break up the larger scraps so that they will melt faster.

3. Heat the double boiler on the stove until the water boils. Turn the heat down, so that the water keeps simmering (just barely bubbling). (Ask permission *before* using the stove!)

4. With the water simmering underneath, the soap scraps will melt. Stir the soap once in a while to help break it down. It may take an hour or so for all the soap to melt. Be patient. (You may need to ask an adult to beat the soap with an electric beater to get all the lumps out.)

5. When the soap is melted, you can add a couple of drops of food coloring.

6. *Very carefully* (the hot soap may burn you if it touches your skin) pour the melted soap into the styrofoam cup. Stop when the cup is half full. Put the two ends of the cord into the soap, keeping the long loop clear of the cup. Then finish filling the cup with soap. Leave it to harden. (If you want it to harden faster, put it into a refrigerator.)

7. When the soap has hardened, peel off the cup. *Voilà*—soap on a rope!

Why Do We Need Soap, Anyway?

Kids sometimes feel that using soap is too much trouble. Why isn't it good enough to wash yourself with water? Your skin has a film of oil on it, and that's where the dirt sticks. Plain water can't wash off this oily dirt, but soapy water can.

Everything in the world is made of tiny bits called *molecules*. Molecules of oil and water just won't stick together. (To prove this to yourself, add a spoonful of cooking oil to a glass of water.)

Since oil and water won't stick together, plain water won't lift oily dirt off your skin. But soap molecules can stick to both oil and water molecules. When you lather soap on your skin, the soap makes a connection between the oil and the water—and they all go down the drain together.

Fingerprint Fun

As far as we know, no two sets of fingerprints are exactly alike. Even identical twins' fingerprints are a little different. Have a look at your own fingerprints and collect some from your friends.

What You Need:
an ink pad with washable ink
sheets of white paper
soft lead pencils
clear sticky tape
family members and/or friends

What to Do:
1. Roll your fingertip from side to side on the ink pad. Then roll your fingertip from side to side on a piece of white paper. You will probably have to practice a few times to get a clear fingerprint. (A little ink is better than a lot. It may help to press your fingertip on the paper with your other hand.)

2. Make a whole set of fingerprints for your right and left hands.

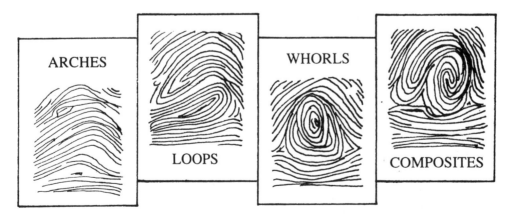

ARCHES

LOOPS

WHORLS

COMPOSITES

3. If you don't have an inkpad, you can still make fingerprints. Rub a soft lead pencil in a small patch on a piece of paper. When you have made a thick, gray place, press your fingertip on it.

4. Now press your fingertip on a short piece of clear sticky tape.

Stick the piece of tape to white paper.

5. The drawing shows the main kinds of fingerprints. Which kind do you have?

6. Collect and compare the fingerprints of some of your family and friends.

Hair-Raising Numbers

Did you know that your hair grows about 2,500 cm (1,000 inches) a day? You have over 100,000 hairs on your head. Each one of them grows about 0.25 mm (1/100 inch) a day—figure it out!

A human hair is so strong that it can be stretched until it is one-third longer, without breaking. The strongest hair ever tested came from a woman in India—it could support 178 g (over 6 ounces). A rope made of just 500 of this woman's hairs would be strong enough to hold the weight of the average man.

Hanging by a Hair

The hairs on your head are a lot stronger than they look. Put a long hair to the test—either your own or somebody else's.

What You Need:
a hair at least 15 cm (6 inches) long
some paperclips, small nails, or screws
tape
a strip of paper about 10 cm long
    and 4 cm wide (about 4 inches
    by 2 inches)

What to Do:

1. Use tape to stick one end of the hair to a shelf or counter, where it can hang free.

2. Make a loop out of the paper. Stick the other end of the hair to the paper loop.

3. Put the nails or paperclips into the loop, one at a time. (All the things you use should be the same size and kind.)

4. How many nails or paperclips can you add before the hair breaks?

5. Try this with hairs from your friends and family. If you want to compare the hairs, always use the same things in the paper loop. Do hairs that look thicker turn out to be stronger? Are curly hairs stronger than straight hairs? Are dark-colored hairs stronger than light-colored hairs?

We tried this with one of Barbara's (straight, brown) hairs. We used "jumbo" paperclips, which are made of thicker wire than the regular kind. They're about 5 cm (2 inches) long. We were able to load on 42 paperclips before the hair broke!

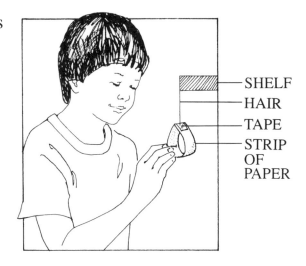

SHELF
HAIR
TAPE
STRIP
OF
PAPER

AMAZING FACTS

Claws!

A man in India holds the record for having the longest fingernails in the world. The five fingernails on his left hand have not been cut since 1952. When measured in 1985, they had a total length of over 363 cm (143 inches). The thumbnail alone measured almost 88 cm (over 34 inches). The man's nails don't look like long daggers, as you might think—they're all twisted around like party streamers.

Spot Some Sweat Glands

You have over 2 million sweat glands in your skin. Find some of the sweat glands on the palms of your hands.

What You Need:
125 mL (½ cup) water
10 mL (2 teaspoons) cornstarch
iodine
measuring cup
measuring spoons
little squares of paper, about 6 cm
   x 6 cm (2½ x 2½ inches)

What to Do:

1. Mix together the water and cornstarch.

2. Dip little squares of paper into the cornstarch-water solution.

3. Paint the palm of your hand with iodine. (Then put the iodine away so that younger children won't find it—it's *poisonous* if swallowed.)

4. Now skip hard, run around the block, or dance to some rock records until you work up a sweat.

5. Press a square of paper to the palm of your hand. What do you see on the paper? Your sweat glands are making these marks.

What Good's a Goosebump?

A goosebump is not much good at all—unless you're a goose! Birds have little muscles in their skin, which let them fluff out their feathers. You can see the bumps of these feather muscles on poultry ready for the oven. Furry animals have the same muscles to let them ruffle their fur. Air is trapped in the fur next to their skin, which helps to keep them warm. Animals' fur also stands up when they see an enemy—it makes them look bigger and stronger.

What about us? Well, we have the same muscles, and we try our best. Each little hair on our bodies stands up when we're cold or really scared. However, our hairs are so fine that they don't help us stay warm or scare off our enemies.

Your Bones

*H*ave you ever seen a human skeleton? Maybe you've seen one in a science museum. Even if you've never looked at a life-size skeleton, you've probably seen cardboard ones hung up as spooky Hallowe'en decorations. Skeletons—especially skulls—are often thought of as scary things. Yet every one of us is walking around with a complete skeleton inside. It's covered by paddings of muscle, fat, and skin.

This framework of bones holds us up and—along with our muscles—lets us move around. It also protects our body organs. Ribs form a cage around our hearts and lungs. Skulls make a hard helmet for our brains.

You can feel a lot of your skeleton by pressing lightly with your fingers. You can trace the jutting brow of your skull and the round sockets for your eyes. Put your fingers just in front of your ears and open and close your mouth. Can you feel the hinge of your jawbone? Press your fingers just under your nose. Open and close your mouth again. Which jawbone moved—the top one or the bottom one?

Run your fingers along your collarbone and breastbone. Count your ribs. Reach behind and touch the bones in your backbone. Keep going, right down to your shinbones, ankles, and toes. How many different bones can you count?

You may be surprised to know that you have well over 200 bones. Many of them are small and can't be felt through your skin. Half of the bones in your body are in your hands and feet. And here's something that may surprise you even more. When you were a baby, you had around 300 bones—but by the time you're grown up, you'll only have 206. How can this be?

As your bones grow, some of the smaller ones will fuse (join together) to make bigger bones. For instance, your backbone has about 33 separate bones (called *vertebrae*). Your parents' backbones only have 26 bones. When you were born, there were still some gaps between the bones in your *cranium* (the top and back of your skull). Slowly these bones grew together, until your cranium looked like one bone. (There are still wiggly lines on it, though, where the eight bones fitted together like jigsaw puzzle pieces.)

When you were born, your bones were quite soft. They had a lot of *cartilage* in them. Cartilage is the rubbery stuff in your nose and outer ears. As bones grow, they get harder, especially on the outside. Minerals, mostly calcium and phosphorus, make your bones much stronger.

Does this mean that bones become hard, dead things—like rocks—as you get older? No, this isn't true at all. Less than half of a bone is made of minerals. Much of the bone is living and growing, with blood vessels running through it. Some bone is very hard. It's called *compact bone*. But your larger bones would be too heavy to lug around if they were made of compact bone all the way through. Many have a lighter, softer part inside, called *spongy bone*. At the center of your biggest bones, like the long bones in your arms and legs, is jelly-like stuff called *marrow*. There are two kinds. Yellow marrow is mostly stored fat. Red marrow makes new red blood cells—about two million cells a second. Your red marrow also makes some kinds of white blood cells.

Where two bones meet, they form a joint. Some joints, like the ones in your cranium, are just glued together. Others—like the ones in your wrists,

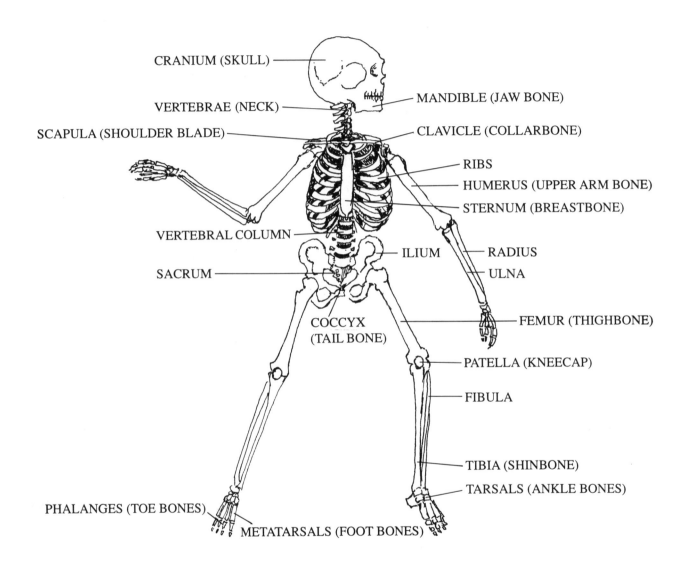

CRANIUM (SKULL)

MANDIBLE (JAW BONE)

VERTEBRAE (NECK)

SCAPULA (SHOULDER BLADE)

CLAVICLE (COLLARBONE)

RIBS

HUMERUS (UPPER ARM BONE)

STERNUM (BREASTBONE)

VERTEBRAL COLUMN

ILIUM

RADIUS

SACRUM

ULNA

COCCYX
(TAIL BONE)

FEMUR (THIGHBONE)

PATELLA (KNEECAP)

FIBULA

TIBIA (SHINBONE)

TARSALS (ANKLE BONES)

PHALANGES (TOE BONES)

METATARSALS (FOOT BONES)

your knees, your hips, and your fingers—need to move. The ends of the bones are covered with smooth cartilage, so that one bone can slip smoothly past another. Special liquid called *synovial fluid* keeps the joints oiled. Tough straps called *ligaments* hold the bones in place.

You have many different kinds of joints. Hinge joints are like the hinges on a door. They only bend in one direction. The elbow is a hinge joint. Can you think of others? Ball and socket joints, like the ones in your hips, let you move more freely. They move like the joysticks on video games.

The only thing still needed by these bones and joints is something to make them move. That something is your muscles—but that's another story!

AMABING FACTS

Bone Record Holders

The largest bone in the human body is the thighbone (femur). All by itself, this bone accounts for over one-quarter of a person's height. The smallest human bone is one of the bones in the inner ear. It's called the *stirrup* because of its shape, and it's only about 3 mm ($\frac{1}{10}$ th of an inch) long. Two or three stirrups could sit on the nail of your baby finger.

The longest bones ever found came from a brachiosaur dinosaur that was dug up in Colorado in the 1970s. The shoulder blades measured 2.4 m (8 feet) long. Some of the ribs were 3 m (10 feet) long. What are the smallest bones in any animal? Probably the tiny ear bones of the bee hummingbird, a bird that is only 2 to 3 cm (1 inch) long. (Why don't we find even tinier bones in insects? The answer is that insects don't have bones at all. Instead they have a hard outer shell called an *exoskeleton*.)

The Original Cast

Feet—they're hardworking, forgotten body parts. Nobody bothers to write songs or poems about them. How about turning yours into works of art?

What You Need:
3 kg (7 pounds) of plaster of Paris (buy at building supply or craft store)
a shoe box
a piece of plastic wrap or aluminum foil
damp sand—enough to fill the shoe box
newspapers
a big empty can
an old spoon or stirring stick
sandpaper

What to Do:
1. Spread out some newspapers where you'll be working. This could get a little messy.

2. Line the shoebox with plastic wrap or aluminum foil.

3. Fill the shoebox about two-thirds full of damp sand. (How damp? As damp as the sand you need to build a sand castle that will hold together—don't make it too watery.)

4. Pour some water into the big can. Stir in plaster of Paris, a little at a time, until the mixture looks like thick cream.

5. Choose your favorite foot. Press that foot straight down into the sand to make a deep, clear footprint. If this doesn't work out, smooth over the sand and try again.

6. Pour the plaster of Paris into the footprint, slowly and evenly. (If the can is too heavy for you, ask an older person to do this step for you.)

7. Leave the plaster to dry. When the plaster is dry, take the plaster foot out and brush off the sand. Use the sandpaper to smooth it. Now you've got a beautiful life-size replica of your foot. What will you do with it? Use your imagination. Could it be a paperweight? A door stopper? Maybe it can be an unusual decoration for your room.

The Incredible Shrinking Kid!

Suppose you asked me how tall I am. Suppose I told you that would depend on what time of day you asked me. Would you think I was crazy? Read on.

What You Need:
a tape measure or metre stick (or yardstick)
a pencil and a notebook
a partner

What to Do:

1. *As soon as you get up in the morning*, stand up straight against a wall, with your feet together. Look straight ahead.

2. Ask your partner to mark your height on the wall with a *very light* pencil mark.

3. Use a metre stick or yardstick (or tape measure) to find out how tall you are. Write it down.

4. Just before you go to bed, measure yourself again in the same way. How tall are you now? Try this for a couple of days in a row. What do you find out?

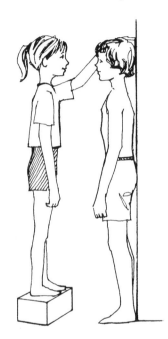

What's Happening?
The hard bones in your spine (vertebrae) have softer "cushions" between them. These are called *discs*. While you jump and twist and turn, your discs keep your vertebrae from getting jolted too much. During the day, gravity

pulls down on your spine . This squeezes some of the water out of the discs. (Gravity is the force that holds you on the earth and keeps you from flying off into space.) So, by bedtime, you're a little shorter than you were in the morning. Overnight, though, the discs fill up with water again .What do you think happens to astronauts who spend a long time in space with no gravity pulling on them?

AMAZING FACTS

The Oldest Human Skulls

Here's the question: "What's the oldest human skull ever found?" It sounds easy to answer, but it's not. The tough word is *human*. At what point do we decide to call ancient bones human? People have not always agreed on this.

The first skull anyone is willing to call *homo* (man) is about 2 million years old. (By the way, *homo* is a Latin word that means people in general, not just men.) This was *Homo habilis* (handy man), who walked on two feet and made very simple stone tools. People have also found skulls of *homo erectus* (upright man), who lived about a million years ago. *Homo erectus* had a bigger brain than *Homo habilis* and knew how to use fire. About 30,000 years ago, skulls of *Homo sapiens sapiens* (people like us) first appeared.

By the way, in all the world, only a few dozen skulls of our most ancient ancestors have been found. People who study dinosaurs have thousands of bones to look at, yet dinosaurs lived much longer ago. Perhaps, a million years ago, there just weren't many people around.

Bend a Bone

Bones are made of both organic material, such as living bones cells and blood vessels, and inorganic material: the minerals that make bones hard. Dissolve (wash away) the minerals and see what's left.

What You Need:
turkey or chicken leg bone
glass jar large enough to hold the bone
strong vinegar

What to Do:

1. Clean all the meat off the leg bone.

2. Put the leg bone in the jar. Pour enough vinegar into the jar to cover the bone.

3. Leave the bone for a few days. Pour off the old vinegar and pour on new vinegar. Do this for two or three weeks.

4. Take the bone out of the vinegar and dry it off. The bone will now bend like a piece of rubber. If it is long enough, you may even be able to tie it in a knot. The vinegar has dissolved most of the hard minerals out of the bone. Without its minerals, the bone is like the rubbery cartilage in your nose.

Your Muscles

*I*t's morning! You hop out of bed, roll up your blind, and blink at the bright sunshine. Where are your slippers? You crawl under your bed and find them. You can smell blueberry pancakes cooking in the kitchen. Good! You're hungry—you can feel your insides gurgling and growling. You hurry down the hall.

You've been up only a couple of minutes and you've used hundreds of muscles already. Muscles in your back, arms, legs, and hands got you out of bed, across your room, and down the hall. But other muscles were at work, too—muscles that you never have to think about. They made the pupils in your eyes (the black centers) smaller when the light hit them. They made your empty stomach churn. They also pushed air in and out of your lungs and kept blood flowing through your body.

You have over 600 muscles. They make up nearly half your weight. Muscles are the "meaty" part of your body, made mostly of protein. In fact, when we eat the meat of animals such as cattle, we're usually eating their muscles.

More than 400 of your muscles work with your bones to move you around. They're called *skeletal* muscles. These muscles are attached to your bones by strong cords called *tendons*. Stretch out your hand and wiggle your fingers. You can see the tendons that reach from the bones in your fingers to the muscles in your wrist and arm.

Muscles can only *pull* a bone. They can't push it. So they often work in pairs. Suppose you want to bend your arm. An upper arm muscle, called the biceps, *contracts*. (This means that it tightens up and gets shorter.) The biceps pulls your arm up. When you want to lower your arm, the biceps relaxes. (This means that it gets longer and flatter.) Another muscle contracts, pulling your arm straight again. This muscle, called the triceps, is on the underside of your upper arm. You can feel your biceps and triceps working. Put your left hand around your upper right arm. Then slowly bend and relax your right arm.

Another name for skeletal muscles is *voluntary* muscles. "Voluntary" means that you can choose whether to move these muscles or not. You decide when you want to stand up, sit down, pick up an apple, or kick a ball. Then your brain sends a signal to your muscles along your nerves, and they get to work.

When you do something over and over again, the muscles work together more smoothly. Then you don't have to think about every little movement. Have you learned how to ride a bicycle? You probably wobbled and shook the first few times you tried. Now you can get on your bicycle and ride off without thinking about how to do it. It's the same when you learn a dance step or play a new sport. The more you practice, the easier it becomes.

Muscles are made of bundles of long fibers (strings). In the big muscle of your behind, the *gluteus maximus*, there might be 200 fibers in a bundle. In your tiny eyelid muscles, there are only about five fibers in a bundle. Each fiber either contracts as tightly as it can, or stays relaxed. It can't contract just a little bit. Yet, when you lift a heavy box, you feel your arm muscles working harder than if you'd picked up an ice cream cone. How can this be?

When you lift the heavy box, a lot of fibers in your arm muscles will contract. When you lift the ice cream cone, only a few will contract. The other muscle fibers will stay relaxed. Each fiber can only contract for a split second. When you need to use a muscle for a long time, the fibers take turns contracting and relaxing. After a while, though, all the fibers will be tired. The muscle will start to tremble and ache, and you have to give it a rest.

Some muscles in your body don't get fatigued (tired) the way voluntary muscles do. These are called *involuntary* muscles, because you don't have to think about working them. They do things like pumping blood through your heart, sucking air into your lungs, and pushing food through your intestines. These actions are just too important to leave to your memory. Imagine how full your day would be if you had no involuntary muscles. Along with remembering to take your lunch and bus fare, go to hockey practice, and do your homework, you'd also have to remember to breathe and digest your food!

Whole Lotta Shakin' Goin' On

The harder you try to hold your arm muscles still, the more little movements they will make.

What You Need:
3 paperclips, or 3 pieces of thin
   wire about 15 cm (6 inches) long
a table knife
a table

What to Do:
1. If you're using paperclips, straighten them out into V shapes. If you're using pieces of wire, fold them in half to form V shapes.

2. Slide the wires onto the smooth edge of the knife blade. Stand beside the table. Hold the knife out in your right hand so that the tips of the wires are just touching the table. (See the drawing.) Don't rest your arm on the table or brace it in any way.

3. Try as hard as you can to keep the knife and the wires still. Are you having any luck? What are those pesky little wires doing?

4. Give your left arm and hand a chance. Do they do any better?

5. Challenge your family or your friends to try this one. Everyone will be surprised at what happens.

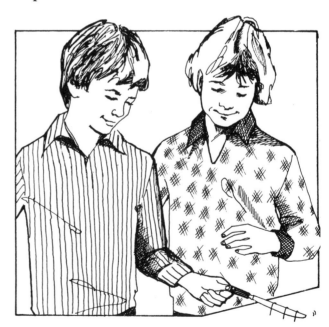

What's Happening?

Inside a muscle, there are always some fibers contracting (tightening up), while others are relaxing. The fibers keep taking turns. Every time they switch over, the muscle twitches a little—so it's impossible for you to hold your arm perfectly still.

AMAZING FACTS

In the Blink of an Eye

The fastest muscle in your body is the one that makes your eyelids open and close. You can blink about 5 times a second. This is not very fast compared to the movements of some other animals. Hummingbirds use their wing muscles to beat their wings about 90 times a second. Insects called *midges* can beat their wings over 1000 times a second—the fastest muscle movement ever recorded!

Challenge Your Muscles

All skeletal muscles get fatigued (tired) when they make the same move over and over. Compare some of your muscles' speed and endurance (ability to keep going).

What You Need:

a clothespeg (the kind that has a
    spring in it)
a hard-cover book that you can lift
    in one hand
a watch or clock that shows
    seconds
paper and pencil

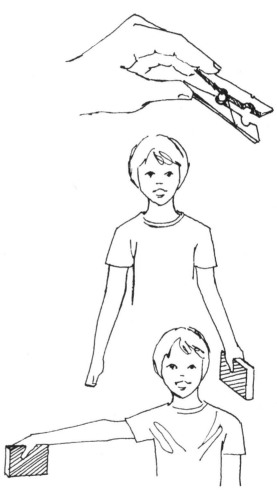

What to Do:

1. First test the muscles in your fingers. Hold the clothespeg between your thumb and index finger. How many times can you squeeze the clothespeg open in 30 seconds? Try this twice more, writing down your score each time. Are you slowing down?

2. Now test the muscles in your hand. Rest your arm on a table, with your palm facing up. Open

and close your hand for 30 seconds. How many times can you do it? Try this twice more, keeping track of your scores.

3. Test the muscles in your arm. Hold your arm straight down, with the book in your hand. Lift your arm to the side, to shoulder height. Lower it again. How many times can you do this in 30 seconds? Try this twice more, keeping track of your scores. Are you slowing down?

If you're right-handed, you probably used your right hand and arm. If you're left-handed, you probably used your left. Try these tests again with your other hand and arm. What do you find out?

Muscle Mystery

Try this one for a weird, floaty feeling.

What You Need:
a doorway to stand in

What to Do:

1. Stand in the doorway with your hands at your sides.

2. Lift your arms until the backs of your hands are touching the door frame on either side.

3. With the backs of your hands and wrists, push against the door frame as hard as you can, counting slowly to 30.

4. Step away from the door frame and let your arms hang loose. What happens?

What's Happening?

Your brain has been sending messages along your nerves to the muscles, telling them to lift your arms. When you suddenly step away from the door, some of those messages are still on their way. It takes a couple of seconds for your muscles to get the latest news—relax.

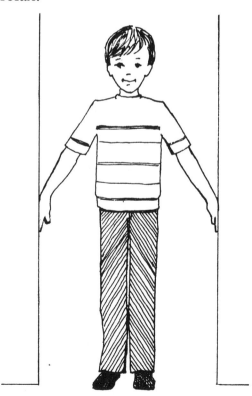

Your Heart and Blood

Try closing your hand into a fist and opening it again. Do this about once a second for a couple of minutes. Your hand will soon feel pretty tired. The muscles need a rest. However, your heart muscle never takes time off, not even when you sleep. When you were a baby, your heart beat about 120 times a minute. As you grew up, this slowed down. An adult's heart beats about 70 times a minute. Even this is faster than you were closing your hand. The only rest your heart muscle ever gets is the little pause between beats.

Your heart is about the size of your fist. It sits in the middle of your chest, between your lungs and behind your ribs and breastbone. Your heart is tipped a little forward on the left side. It has a thick wall down the middle, called the *septum*, and it has four chambers (spaces). The top chambers are called *atria*, and the bottom ones are called *ventricles*. Between the atria and ventricles are little trap doors called *valves*. Your heart is a powerful pump. As your heart muscle contracts (squeezes), it pumps blood through its chambers and out into your body.

This is how it goes: Blood comes into your *right* atrium through two tubes called *veins*. This blood has been all over your body—in your fingers, toes, brain, and intestines. The valve opens, and the blood flows down into the right ventricle. Your heart gives a squeeze. This pushes the blood out of the ventricle into a tube called an *artery*. The artery carries it to your lungs. From your lungs, the blood travels back to your heart. This time it enters the *left* atrium. It goes through the valve into the left ventricle. This time, when your heart squeezes, the blood rushes out into a large artery that starts it on a trip to all parts of your body.

What's in this blood that your heart is pumping? Why does your body need blood anyway? A little over half your blood is liquid called *plasma*. It carries nutrients (tiny broken-down bits of food) to all parts of your body. Your blood is also the "stream" that carries your blood cells along. Nearly all of these are red blood cells.

Under a microscope, a red blood cell looks like a little saucer with a dip in the middle. But think of red blood cells as tiny cargo boats. They arrive at your heart (the right side, remember) carrying carbon dioxide, a waste gas that your body wants to get rid of. Your heart sends them on to your lungs. In your lungs, the red blood cells drop off the carbon dioxide (which you breathe out). They pick up a fresh load of a gas called oxygen (which you just breathed in). Then they go back to the heart (the left side). From there, they are pumped out again to all parts of your body, where the oxygen is needed.

You also have white blood cells, but not nearly as many as red cells. There's one white cell for every 500 to 1000 red cells. White cells are bigger than red ones. White cells cruise around your blood like an army, protecting you from attack by germs. One kind of white cell can even gobble up things that shouldn't stay in your blood, like bacteria or old dead blood cells.

Besides red and white cells, you also have lots of broken cell bits called *platelets* in your blood. If you cut your finger, the platelets catch on the rough edges of the cut. They spill out a chemical that helps to make little sticky threads. The threads form a *clot* to patch the cut. This keeps you from losing too much blood.

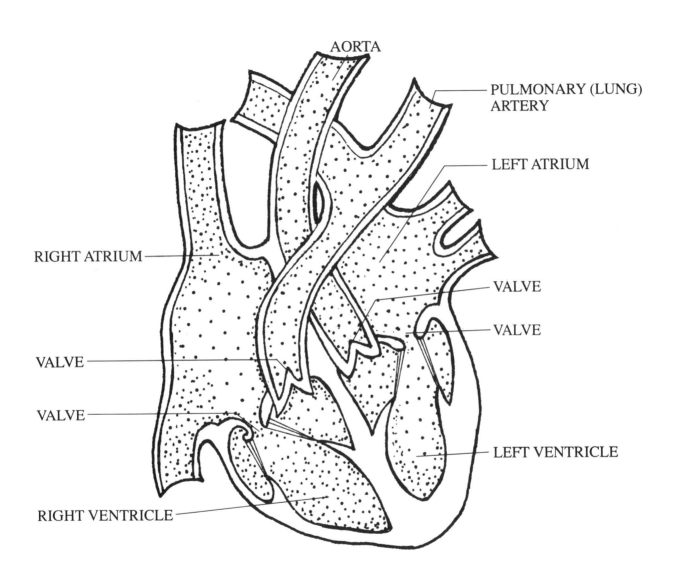

AORTA

PULMONARY (LUNG) ARTERY

LEFT ATRIUM

RIGHT ATRIUM

VALVE

VALVE

VALVE

VALVE

LEFT VENTRICLE

RIGHT VENTRICLE

Your blood travels around your body through a huge branching network of blood vessels. There are three kinds: arteries, veins, and capillaries. Arteries carry blood away from your heart. They must have thick, muscular walls, because blood rushes through them in great waves pumped by your heart. At a few places in your body—such as your wrists and your neck—arteries are close enough to your skin that you can feel the pumping. This pumping is called your *pulse*.

The arteries branch into smaller and smaller vessels until at last they are tiny *capillaries*. Some capillaries are so small that the blood cells have to squeeze through in single file! The walls of capillaries are so thin that nutrients and gases can pass right through into the body cells that need them.

Your blood journeys back to the heart through your veins. Veins can have thinner walls, since the blood doesn't pulse as hard through them as through arteries. Some veins—like those in your legs—work against gravity (the force that pulls us down towards the earth). They have little valves in them to keep the blood from flowing back the wrong way. Smaller veins join bigger ones, like small streams flowing into a bigger one. Finally the biggest veins of all pour the blood back into your heart.

The whole incredible trip that your blood makes—from heart to lungs, back to the heart, out to the body, and back to the heart again—takes about 23 seconds!

And The Winner Is—Us

A shrew—a tiny, fierce relative of the mouse—has a heart that beats about 1000 times a minute. It lives about 1½ years. A rabbit's heart beats about 200 times a minute. It lives about 6 years. An elephant's heart beats about 25 times a minute. It lives about 60 years. If you take the trouble to do the multiplication, you'll find out that each of these mammals gets between 500 million and a billion (1000 million) heartbeats in its lifetime. (For example, the rabbit gets 200 beats a minute x 60 minutes in an hour x 24 hours in a day x 365 days a year x 6 years.) This is about average for mammals.

The smaller mammals tend to live fast and die young. The bigger ones have slower heartbeats and last longer. But what about human beings, who are also mammals? People live to be about 70, and their hearts beat about 70 times a minute. This means that human hearts beat about 2.5 billion times before they give out.

The Beat Goes On

As your heart beats and sends a wave of blood through your body, you can feel this in your arteries. It's called your *pulse*. Your wrist is a good place to feel and see your pulse.

What You Need:
a watch that shows seconds
a small piece of Plasticine
a toothpick

What to Do:

1. This is how to take your pulse. Put the three middle fingers of one hand on the inside of your other wrist. Rest your fingertips against the thumb side of your wrist. You will feel a regular throbbing under your fingers. This is your pulse beat.

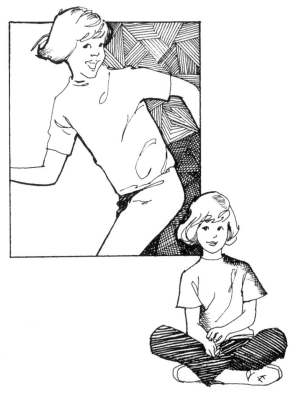

2. Sit in a chair resting for about 5 minutes. Now count the beats in your wrist for one minute. That is your pulse rate. A kid's pulse rate is usually in the range of 90 to 120 beats a minute. An adult's pulse rate is slower— around 70 beats a minute.

3. Try running or skipping for a couple of minutes and then take your pulse again. What has happened?

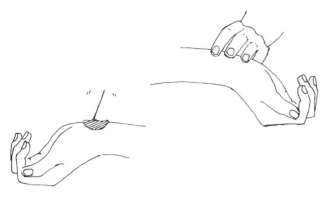

4. Now try taking the pulses of some other members of your family. What do you find out?

5. To see your pulse beat, make a pulse meter. Take a little ball of Plasticine, about the size of a marble. Flatten it just enough so that it will sit on your wrist. Stick a toothpick in it. When you set the pulse meter on your wrist pulse point, the toothpick will bob back and forth in time to the beat.

This doesn't work for everyone all the time. I can get a pulse meter to bob on one wrist, but not on the other. Move your meter around to a couple of spots on the inside of your wrist before you give up. Watch carefully for the back and forth movement. Try it on friends and family members. When it works, it's fun to see.

6. You might also like to count how fast your pet's heart beats. You can usually feel the heartbeat of a cat or dog by placing your hand on the pet's chest, below the left front leg. You can feel the rapid heartbeats of small rodent pets like guinea pigs when you're holding them. Be *gentle*—don't squeeze!

Lub-DUB, Lub-DUB

Doctors use a stethoscope to listen to people's hearts. You can make a simple stethoscope and hear heart sounds for yourself.

What You Need:
two funnels
a piece of rubber or plastic tubing
  that will fit into the small ends of
  the funnels, about 60 cm (24 inches) long. Note: Aquarium
  tubing, sold in pet stores, is
  cheap and easy to use.
a friend to work with

What to Do:
1. Fit the small ends of the two funnels over the ends of the plastic tubing.

2. Go to a *quiet* place. Put the large end of one funnel on your friend's chest, a little to the left of center. Hold the large end of the other funnel to your ear. Can you hear your friend's heartbeat? You may have to move the stethoscope a couple of times to find the best spot.

3. Have your friend jog on the spot for a moment, and listen again. What has happened?

4. Trade places and let your friend listen in on your heart.

What's Happening?
People often describe the heart sounds as "lub-DUB." The lub is the sound of the valves between the atria and the ventricles closing. The louder DUB is the sound of the valves at the top the heart closing. These shut off the big blood vessels leaving the heart.

AMAZING FACTS

Blood Count

- An average adult man has about 5 to 6 L (10 to 12 pints) of blood. An average woman has about 4 to 5 L (8 to 10 pints). The heart circulates this blood more that 1,000 times a day.
- If all the body's blood vessels were laid end to end, they would stretch 96,000 km (60,000 miles). That's about two and a half times around the world.
- The largest arteries and veins are about 2.5 cm (1 inch) across. The smallest capillaries are much finer than a human hair.
- An adult has about 35,000,000,000,000 (35 trillion) red blood cells. Each cell lives about 4 months. Before it wears out, it makes about 160,000 trips to and from the heart.

Discover Some Blood Vessels

You've probably noticed a few branching blood vessels under your skin—perhaps on the inner side of your wrist or elbow. Here are some blood vessels you may not have looked at before.

What You Need:
a mirror
a penlight (a small flashlight)

What to Do:

1. You need a mirror with good overhead light—perhaps the bathroom mirror.

2. Prepare yourself for a strange sight. Curl up your tongue and have a look at the underside. You never suspected *that* was in your mouth, did you! Your tongue is a big muscle, fed by lots of blood vessels. The thick blue ones are veins. The thick pink ones are arteries. The little branching red threads are capillaries, the smallest blood vessels.

3. Another good place to see little capillaries is in your eyelid. Gently pull down your lower lid and have a look.

4. You can even see blood vessels *inside* your eye—but you have to be clever about it. Go into a dark room. Close your eyes. Turn on the penlight, and touch it gently to your eyelid near the outside corner of one eye. Jiggle the penlight. You will see a mysterious branching pattern, like a spooky leafless tree. What you're really seeing are the blood vessels at the back of your eye.

5. Do you want to see blood pulsing along the little capillaries in your eyes? You need a clear blue sky. Close one eye and gaze at the sky with the other. (*Don't* look at the sun, though—just the sky.) You should see small, bright dots keeping time with your heartbeat.

AMAZING FACTS

Antibodies to the Rescue

Some of your white blood cells are on a special patrol. They're looking for viruses—very tiny germs that can get into your body and make you sick. On the outsides of these white cells are *antibodies*. They are little bits of chemical with special shapes. These shapes are like keys looking for just the right lock. The lock is on the enemy virus.

When the white cell meets a certain kind of enemy virus, it makes a lot more antibodies to fit that kind of virus. They lock into the viruses and stop them from spreading. Then other white cells come along and eat the viruses up. What's even better is that some of the antibodies stay in your blood, ready for the next attack. If the same kind of virus tries to get you again, it will be outnumbered right away.

When you have a shot to *immunize* you against a disease like measles or polio, you are given some weakened or killed viruses. They still seem like dangerous enemies, and your body makes antibodies against them. Later, if the real viruses try to make you sick, the antibodies in your blood will be ready to stop them.

Your Lungs

Sometimes, when I was a kid, I would see how long I could hold my breath. After a minute or so, my lungs would feel as if they were going to burst! Soon I'd have to take a breath. I can still remember how great that first big gasp of air always felt.

Most of the time, of course, we don't think about breathing. But, like most living creatures, we need to breathe a gas called *oxygen*. We need it to burn our body fuel—the food that we eat. Our lungs are built to take oxygen out of the air. Fish have gills that can take oxygen out of water.

Every minute, even when you're asleep, you breathe in and out about 15 or 20 times. (You breathe faster if you're running or jumping.) You don't need to remember to breathe. This is a lucky thing. You could survive for weeks without food if you had to. You could survive for days without water. But you could live only a few minutes without oxygen.

Breathing starts in your nose and mouth. If your nose is plugged with a cold, you can use just your mouth to breathe. If you do this, though, you'll find that your throat starts to get dry and scratchy. Your nose works better for breathing. That's because it makes the air wet and warm before it goes any farther into your body. Your nose also has bristly hairs and sticky mucus (the stuff that comes out of your nose when you blow it). These trap dust and bacteria.

The passages from your nose and your mouth meet at your *pharynx* (throat). Two passages lead down from your pharynx. One is for food and the other—called the *trachea* or windpipe—is for air. The trachea has a "trap door" at its top—the *epiglottis*. The epiglottis snaps shut when food is coming down. Every once in awhile, especially if you're laughing and talking while eating, a crumb of food manages to "go down the wrong way." Then a cough—a high-speed rush of air from your lungs—blasts it back up again.

The trachea is like the trunk of a spreading, upside-down tree. This "tree" fills your chest from your collarbone to the bottom of your ribs. The trunk divides into two main branches called *bronchi*. Each of these branches leads to a lung. Inside your lungs, the bronchi spread into many smaller branches, called *bronchioles*. At the ends of the smallest twigs, instead of leaves, there are clusters of tiny balloons. These balloons are called *alveoli*. There are hundreds of millions of them in your lungs. If they could all be spread out flat, they'd take up an area about 25 times the size of your skin.

The air you breathe in finally ends up in your alveoli. The alveoli are surrounded by small blood vessels. The walls of the alveoli are so thin that gases can pass right through them into your blood. The blood vessels pick up the gas called oxygen, and carry it to every part of your body. They also drop off wastes that your body wants to get rid of—a gas called carbon dioxide and also water vapor. (On a wintry day, stand close to a cold window and breathe on it. You'll see the water droplets form as you breathe out.)

A big muscle called the *diaphragm* is spread out under your lungs. When it contracts (tightens up), it pulls down a bit. Then your ribs move outward, your lungs expand (get bigger), and air is sucked in. When your diaphragm relaxes, air is pushed out.

We breathe in and out thousands of times every day. If the air we breathe is polluted—poisonous or dirty—then some of the poison and dirt end up in our lungs. We can all work for cleaner air, by joining anti-pollution groups, or by sending letters (or drawings or poems) to the government to let them know how we feel.

One important thing you can do for yourself is decide not to smoke. There's no doubt any more that smoking is a cause of lung cancer and other lung diseases. (It isn't good for blood vessels and hearts, either.) Take a deep breath on a bright, beautiful morning. Aren't you feeling great? Take care of your lungs so that all your mornings will feel as wonderful as this one.

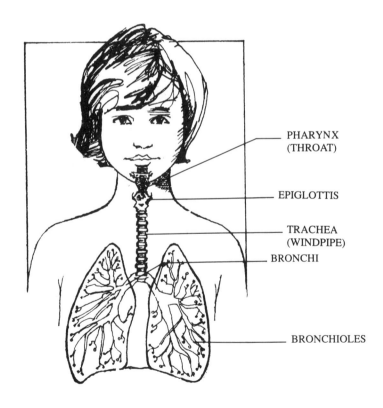

PHARYNX
(THROAT)

EPIGLOTTIS

TRACHEA
(WINDPIPE)

BRONCHI

BRONCHIOLES

What a Blast!

A sneeze is a pretty hard thing to stop. When anything gets into your nose that shouldn't be there, such as dust or bacteria, your body makes you sneeze it out. Sneezing is a reflex, like coughing or blinking—something you do without even thinking about it.

First your mouth opens and you take in a big breath of air—AAHHHH! Then your chest muscles squeeze. Air rushes up from your lungs and out your nose at a very high speed—CHOOO! Sneezes have been measured at over 160 km/h (100 mph). This is much faster than cars travel on North American highways; faster than the speediest fastball in the major leagues; and faster than Wayne Gretzky's best shot!

A Breathtaking Model

Build a model that shows how your lungs work.

What You Need:
a bottle made of soft clear plastic
2 balloons
a piece of Plasticine
a plastic drinking straw
a small elastic band
scissors

What to Do:

 1. Cut away the base of the bottle. (You may have to ask a grown-up to do this for you.)

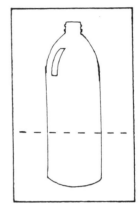

2. Knot one balloon. Cut off the other end of the balloon. Stretch the rest of the balloon over the end of the bottle.

3. Fit the end of the other balloon over the end of the drinking straw. Hold it in place with the elastic band.

4. Then push the straw and balloon through the opening of the bottle, so that the balloon is inside the bottle.

5. Seal the opening of the bottle with Plasticine. (Or, if the bottle has a plastic cap, you might be able to make a hole in the cap and thread the straw through it.) The opening must be airtight, except for the straw.

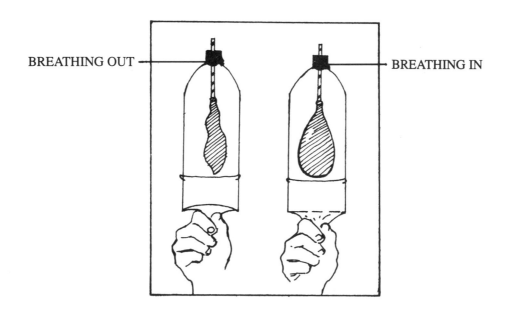

BREATHING OUT — | — BREATHING IN

6. Push up on the balloon stretched over the bottle. What do you see? Now pull down on the balloon. What do you see? Hold the straw near your face. What do you feel as you push and pull the balloon?

What's Happening?

This is a model of the way you breathe. The bottle is like your chest, and the balloon across the bottom of the bottle is like your diaphragm. The balloon inside the bottle is like one of your lungs, and the straw is like the bronchial tube that leads to your lungs. When you push up on the "diaphragm," your balloon lung shrinks and air comes out the straw. This is what happens when you breathe out. When you pull down on the diaphragm, air is sucked into the "lung" and fills it. This is like what happens when you breathe in.

Can You Puff Enough?

How big a breath can you take in and blow out? Here's a way to find out.

What You Need:

a big, clear plastic jug that will hold about 4 L (1 gallon)

a piece of plastic or rubber tubing, about 90 cm (36 inches) long

a bathroom sink with a plug

a marker pen that can write on the jug

a measuring cup

a pencil and notebook

a partner

What to Do:

1. Use the measuring cup to fill the jug with water. Every time you pour 500 mL (2 cups) into the jug, make a mark on the side of the jug to show where the water reaches. Keep going until you fill the jug, marking off every 500 mL.

2. Put the plug in the sink. Fill the sink about ⅔ full of water.

3. Place your hand firmly over the mouth of the jug so no water can escape. Right away, turn the jug upside down in the sinkful of water. Take your hand away. The water should stay in the jug. (If the jug is too heavy for you or your hand can't cover the mouth of the jug, ask an older person to do this for you. You can do the next step.)

4. Ask your partner to hold the jug. Put one end of the tubing inside the mouth of the jug. Let the jug rest on the bottom of the sink (your partner will have to keep holding it) so that the tubing will stay put.

5. Put the other end of the tubing in your mouth. Exhale. (That means "breathe out.")

6. The air you breathe out bubbles into the jug. Water is forced out of the jug. Look at the markings on the side of the jug and see how much you exhaled. Write it down in your notebook.

7. Fill the jug again and let your partner try.

8. Fill the jug again. This time, take a couple of deep breaths before you start. Take a final BIG breathe and exhale into the tube. How close can you come to emptying the jug?

The most air an adult can breathe out in one big breath is 4 or 5 L (about a gallon). Most of the time, people breathe out only about 0.5 L (a pint) of air in one breath. Remember that children have smaller lungs and take smaller breaths.

Your Digestive System

What's your favorite meal? Cabbage rolls? Pasta? Shrimp curry? What's your favorite dessert? Chocolate pudding? Baklava? Cheese and crackers? If you live in a country with enough good food to eat, you're lucky. Mealtimes are one of life's pleasures.

Your body doesn't really care whether you like hamburgers or pork chops, oranges or strawberries. It needs food, but in forms that you never see on a restaurant menu. Your body needs *carbohydrates* (sugars and starches). It can get these from fruit, milk, and bread, for instance. Your body needs *proteins*, which are in meat, fish, eggs, cheese, and other foods. It needs *fats*, which are in such foods as butter, nuts, and meat. It also needs tiny bits of *vitamins* and *minerals*, and lots of water.

Your digestive system is a long tube that goes right through your body. By the time you're grown up, it will be about 8 m (26 feet) long. How can such a long tube fit inside you? A lot of it is neatly coiled, like a garden hose. The job of the digestive system is to break down the food you eat into little bits that your body cells can use.

As soon as you put some food in your mouth, digestion starts. Your teeth tear and grind the food into smaller pieces. Saliva flows in from glands near your mouth and makes the food mushy. Saliva has an *enzyme* in it (a body chemical that breaks down food). This enzyme goes to work on the carbohydrates right away. Then your tongue flips the food to the back of your mouth and you swallow. There, you've done the part you have to think about. Digestion will carry on while you read a book, play a game—even while you sleep.

When you swallow, the food doesn't just fall down into your stomach. It's squeezed down by the muscles in your *esophagus*. This is a 25 cm (10 inch) tube that leads to your stomach. Once you swallow food, it'll work its way through the digestive system even if you're standing on your head!

Put your hand on your stomach. Did you put your hand on your navel (also known as your belly button)? Many people make this mistake. But your stomach is really much higher, under your bottom ribs. When your stomach is empty, it's like a big J-shaped sausage. After a big meal, when it's full of food, it looks more like a football.

Food takes only a few seconds to go down your esophagus. Then things slow down a lot. Your stomach doesn't pass your meal along until it's made a lot of changes to the food. The walls of your stomach are muscles that can squeeze in three different directions. They shake and churn the food until it's well mixed. Your stomach also adds a strong acid to the

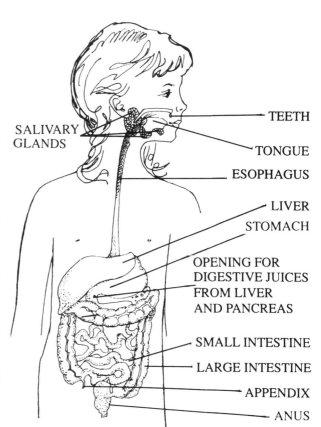

SALIVARY GLANDS

TEETH

TONGUE

ESOPHAGUS

LIVER

STOMACH

OPENING FOR DIGESTIVE JUICES FROM LIVER AND PANCREAS

SMALL INTESTINE

LARGE INTESTINE

APPENDIX

ANUS

food. This acid is good at breaking up protein. It turns your meal into a very sour soup. (When you've eaten something that makes you sick, this is the stuff you throw up.)

At the bottom of your stomach is a sphincter (a ring of muscle). Every few minutes, it opens and squirts some food into the small intestine. Three to five hours are needed for a whole meal to pass through the stomach.

The small intestine is a long coiled tube, about 6.5 m (21 feet) long. For about five hours, the food is squeezed through the small intestine. This is where most of your digestion takes place. Digestive juices flow in from two important body organs: your *liver* and your *pancreas*. The liver makes thick green *bile*, which breaks down fats. The pancreas makes a juice full of enzymes to break down sugar, protein, and fat.

The walls of the small intestine are lined with millions of *villi*, which look like tiny waving fingers. Each one has many capillaries (blood vessels finer than hairs) going through it. Nutrients (broken down food bits) can pass right through the walls of the villi into the capillaries. The capillaries carry them to all parts of your body. Hours after you swallowed your meal, your body cells are finally fed!

Any food that still hasn't been digested moves on to your large intestine. It's bigger around than your small intestine, but much shorter—only about 1.5 m (5 feet) long. The large intestine looks something like an upside-down, U-shaped sausage. It leads out of your body through a sphincter muscle opening called the *anus*. The large intestine takes as much water out of the leftovers as it can. What's left is a brown sludge called *feces* (and other, less polite names). Now comes the only other part of digestion you have to think about. You make a trip to the bathroom and push out the wastes.

Enzymes in Action

Did you know that digestion actually starts in your mouth? Give your enzymes something to work on—you'll see and taste what they do.

I. Cracker Crunch

What You Need:
soda cracker or half-slice of bread

What to Do:
Chew up the soda cracker or the bread. Hold it in your mouth for 5 minutes. (Your mouth will fill up with spit "soup," but try not to swallow!) How does the taste of the cracker or bread change?

II. Spit and Demolish

What You Need:
baby food jar of strained corn

What to Do:
Add a couple of drops of saliva (spit) to a jar of strained corn baby food. Leave the jar on the kitchen counter overnight. In the morning, have a look. Eccch! What has happened? (Needless to say, you won't be feeding this to any babies in your family!)

What's Happening?
The saliva in your mouth contains an enzyme called *amylase*. *Enzymes* are chemicals that break down food so your body can use it. Amylase has the special job of breaking down starch into sugar. That's what happened to the starchy cracker when you held it in your mouth. A little of your saliva in the baby food broke down its starch, turning it into a soupy mess.

See Vitamin C

Vitamin C is just one of the vitamins we need. It keeps our gums healthy and helps cuts to heal. Test some fruit juices and other drinks to find out how much Vitamin C they have.

What You Need:
a kettle
a 250 mL (1 cup) measuring cup
cornstarch
iodine
an eyedropper
a drinking glass
a spoon
some canned juices, freshly
    squeezed orange or lemon
    juice, and fruit-flavored
    powdered drinks
a pencil and notebook

What to Do:

1. *Don't do this step without a grownup standing by.* Boil some water in a kettle. When the water is boiling, pour it into a 250 mL (1 cup) measuring cup.

2. Stir 5 mL (1 teaspoon) of cornstarch into the cup of water.

3. Use the eyedropper to add iodine to the water, a couple of drops at a time. While you add the iodine, stir the water with a spoon. Keep adding iodine until the water turns blue. This is your Vitamin C tester.

4. Put away the iodine. It's harmless to use in this test, but it's poison if it's swallowed. You want to keep it away from younger kids who might try to taste it.

5. Wash out the eyedropper, because you're going to need it again.

6. Pour a little bit of your tester into a drinking glass. Use the eyedropper to add some juice to the glass, one drop at a time.

How many drops does it take to 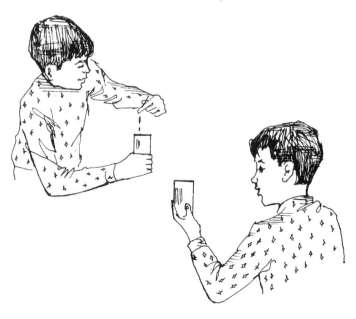 make the blue color disappear? Write down the number of drops. The *more* Vitamin C there is in the juice, the *fewer* drops it will take to make the blue disappear.

7. Try the test again with other glasses of tester and other juices. Try some canned orange juice and some freshly squeezed orange juice. Which seems to have more Vitamin C? Try a drink labeled "orange drink." Does it have any Vitamin C?

8. What happens to Vitamin C when it's heated? Find out by boiling a little orange juice in a saucepan. (Use one of the kinds of orange juice that you used in Step 7.) Add it to the tester with the eyedropper. Is there any Vitamin C?

9. Leave a glass of orange juice standing on a counter for two days. Then try the test. Is there any Vitamin C?

Does all this give you some ideas about the best way to get your Vitamin C?

No-Bake, Hands-On Power Snacks

Why settle for junk food, when you can have a snack that's delicious and good for you, too? These are easy to fix—you roll them with your hands like Plasticine.

What You Need:

60 mL (¼ cup) butter
60 mL (¼ cup) peanut butter
125 mL (½ cup) honey
5 mL (1 teaspoon) vanilla
375 mL (1½ cups) quick-cooking rolled oats
125 mL (½ cup) toasted wheat germ
85 mL (⅓ cup) nonfat dry milk powder
30 mL (2 tablespoons) unsweetened cocoa powder
0.5 mL (⅛ teaspoon) ground cinnamon
sesame seeds and chopped nuts

measuring cups and spoons
a saucepan
a stirring spoon
a cookie sheet
wax paper

What to Do:

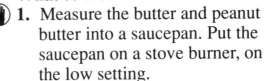

1. Measure the butter and peanut butter into a saucepan. Put the saucepan on a stove burner, on the low setting.

2. Keep stirring the butter and peanut butter mixture with a spoon until it's melted. Take the saucepan off the stove. (Remember to turn off the burner!)

3. Stir in the honey and vanilla. Then stir in the oats, wheat germ, milk powder, cocoa, and cinnamon until they're all well mixed together. (It's not a bad idea to read the list again, to see if you've left out anything.)

4. Put some sesame seeds and finely chopped nuts on a piece

of wax paper. Cover the cookie sheet with another piece of wax paper.

5. Use your hands to roll out "snakes" of dough about 1 cm (½ inch) thick and about 7 cm (3 inches) long.

6. Roll your snakes—er, snacks— in the seeds and nuts to coat them. Then put them on the cookie sheet. When all your snacks are made, put the cookie sheet in the refrigerator for about 2 hours. (Or until they're firm enough to pick up and eat.) Yum! Keep any leftovers in a covered container.

AMAZING FACTS

Grumbling in Greek

It's happened to all of us at one time or another. If you're unlucky, it happens in a very quiet place where other people can hear it. Your poor hungry insides start to growl and gurgle. Your digestive system is squeezing and churning, just as if it had food in it. But all it has to work with are gas and digestive juices. You feel as if the sounds are coming from your stomach—but more likely they're coming from your intestines. If you're embarrassed you can turn to the person next to you and say very calmly, "I'm *so* sorry. My borborygmus is acting up again." What's *borborygmus*? It's a fancy medical word that comes from Greek. It means—a tummy grumble.

Eating Out—Starfish Style

Most animals digest their food inside their bodies, usually in some kind of long tube. However, the starfish has another way. Its favorite food is clam. The starfish has no teeth or claws to break open the clam's thick shell— but it doesn't have to. Instead, the starfish presses its mouth to the little gap where the two halves of the clamshell meet. (Did you ever wonder where a starfish has its mouth? It's on the underside, at the center of its arms.) The starfish pushes its stomach out of its mouth and *right inside* the clam's shell. Then it digests the clam. The starfish takes about three days to eat its dinner. When it's finished, it swallows its stomach and sidles off.

Your Brain and Nerves

What is your brain doing for you right now? The short answer is: everything! Your brain is the master control center of your body. It allows you to read and understand this book. At the same time, it's controlling your heartbeat, your breathing, and many other body activities. Your brain is locked away inside a safety vault of bone—your skull. But it keeps in touch with everything that's happening inside you and around you. A long spinal cord and a huge branching network of nerves join your brain to every other part of your body.

An adult's brain weighs about 1.4 kg (under 3 pounds). More than three-quarters of this is taken up by the *cerebrum*. The cerebrum is divided into two halves, or *hemispheres*. The wrinkled, folded outside part of the cerebrum is called the *cerebral cortex*.

The cerebral cortex takes care of thinking and remembering. People who study the brain still don't know how we remember. They know, though, that there are different kinds of memory. *Short-term memory* lasts only long enough to let you do things like dial a phone number you just looked up. *Long-term memory* lets you store information longer.

The cerebral cortex receives nerve messages from your eyes, ears, and touch sensors in your skin. It decides what to do about them. Then it returns messages along other nerves that make your muscles move. The nerves from your body cross as they go into your brain. (No one knows why.) This means that the left side of your cortex controls the right side of your body. The right side of the cortex looks after your left side.

For some jobs, the hemispheres *specialize* (divide up the work). The left hemisphere, for instance, is in charge of speaking and learning languages. The right side is good at judging distances and shapes, and drawing. People who study the brain think some human beings may have their brainwork divided up differently. There are still many things about the human brain that we do not understand.

Tucked under the cerebrum at the back of your brain is the *cerebellum*. It takes care of balance and making your muscles work well together.

Deep inside your brain, under the cerebrum, are small but important parts belonging to the *limbic system*. One of these parts, the *hypothalamus*, keeps your body at the right temperature, tells you when you're hungry and thirsty, puts you to sleep, and wakes you up. It also makes you feel strong emotions like fear and anger. All this is pretty amazing for something the size of a pea!

At the back and bottom of your brain is your *brainstem*. This is where messages from your nerves first enter your brain. Part of the brainstem sorts through the messages and "decides" where they should go. The brainstem also looks after your breathing and heartbeat, without bothering the higher parts of your brain. You don't have to think about these things.

Your *spinal cord* is a thick cable of nerves running up your back and into your brain. It is protected by a chain of knobby bones called *vertebrae*. Between the vertebrae are small spaces where nerves pass through. These branching nerves go everywhere in your body. Some nerves carry messages from your cerebrum and cerebellum. They work your voluntary muscles (the ones you have to think about moving). Some nerves carry messages from the brainstem. They work the muscles you don't have to think about. These are the ones that pump your blood, squeeze food in your stomach, and so on. Other nerves carry messages back to your brain. They tell the brain what's going on out there in the rest of your body.

Some nerve messages don't go any farther than your spinal cord. These are called *reflexes*. Suppose, by accident, you lift a hot pot from the stove. Your hand jerks back before you even have time to think. As soon as the heat warning reaches your spinal cord, it sends a message back: *drop it!* If you had to wait for a message to go all the way to your brain, you might be burned before the brain sent its reply.

Nerves are made up of spidery looking cells called *neurons*. Each neuron has a lot of little threads running out of it, called *dendrites*. Each neuron also has one very long thread, the *axon*. Nerve messages go from the axon of a neuron to one dendrite of another neuron. The message travels as a little electrical signal, but it also needs special brain chemicals to help it along.

How many neurons do we have? The guesses range from 10 billion to 100 billion. (A billion is a thousand million.) Although we are learning more and more about how the brain works, we still have many mysteries to solve. It's interesting to think we're using our brains to solve puzzles about—themselves!

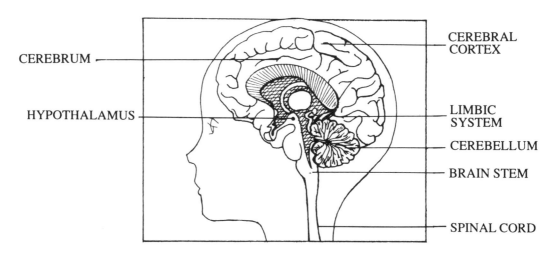

Mighty Memory

Before people had written languages, ancient storytellers trained themselves to recite very long stories and poems from memory. The stories were handed down from older people to younger ones, so that they wouldn't be lost. You can train your memory just as the storytellers did, by paying attention and hearing something over and over. But this game isn't hard work, it's lots of fun.

What You Need:
at least one other person to play with—a group of four or five is even more fun

What to Do:
1. One person begins, "I packed my suitcase with a . . . swimsuit" (or anything else the person wants to say).

2. The second person repeats what the first person said, and adds something: "I packed my suitcase with a swimsuit. . . and a watermelon."

3. Third person: "I packed my suitcase with a swimsuit, a watermelon, and a boa constrictor." And so on.

4. Each person has to recite *everything* that was listed, *in the right order*. Whoever misses has to drop out. (The first dropout might like to keep a list of what people say. Then if everyone starts to forget, or there's a disagreement about what was said, people can check the list.)

What's interesting about this game is that people will usually remember the first few things on the list very well—they've heard them said over and over. People are likelier to miss the thing that was "packed" just before their own turn.

It's interesting to hear what people do and say to help themselves remember—it shows you something about how other people's brains work. People will screw up their faces, close their eyes, or tap their foreheads as they think hard. One person who has forgotten something will say, "I know it begins with 'g'!" Another person will say, "I know it was some kind of animal—but which one?" Some people will start the whole list over, trying to "sneak up" on the forgotten thing and tease it out of their brains that way.

Some people who study the brain use games like this to try to understand how people think. Computer scientists are also very interested in how people remember things, because they would like to program computers to "think" like human beings.

Make a Mental Picture

Your fingers can give your brain a "mental picture" of something your eyes can't see.

What You Need:
coins: a quarter, a nickel, a dime,
   a penny (add a dollar coin if you
   have one)
a partner

What to Do:

1. Put the coins in your pockets (or in a soft bag that you can't see through).

2. Put your hand in with the coins. Without looking, feel the coins. Push them around with your fingers. Can you tell which is which?

3. Ask your partner to name one of the coins and see if you can pull out the right one. Keep doing this until your pocket is empty. Now let your partner try. How did each of you do?

4. Now lay the coins on the table in a line. Close your eyes. Ask your partner to change the order of the coins so that you don't know which coin is where.

5. Touch the coins with a fingertip. You may touch the tops and the edges, but you may not pick them up. Try to guess which coin you're touching.

What's Happening?

You probably found it much harder to tell the coins apart on the table. When they were in your pocket, you could: move them around, feel their weight, touch them on all sides, and compare them with each other. From all the information that the nerve receptors in your fingers sent back, your brain built up a mental picture of what was in your pocket. People who study the brain call this *haptic touch*.

How Strong Are Habits?

Habits save us a lot of time every day. When we are first learning, we do things slowly, step by step. As they become habits, we can do them in one quick, flowing motion. Look at some of your habits.

I. T's Tease

What You Need:
sheets of paper and pencils
family or friends (you can do this
   on your own, but it's more fun in
   a group)

What to Do:
1. One person reads the following sentences out loud. The others write them down, going as fast as they can. Here's the catch: the writers must not cross any t's or dot any i's. Here are the sentences:
   - Is this a trick or is this a test?
   - Two tiny twins took their toys to the inn.
   - I like cider with ice. I sip it through a straw.
   - This little kitten has lost its mittens.
   - It was misty and rain hit the window.

2. You probably found that the writers crossed a few t's and dotted a few i's, even though they were trying not to. This is a trick that grownups often find harder than kids do. Their habits are stronger, because they've been writing for many years. Kids, who haven't been writing for as long, go more slowly. They have to pay more attention. They may find it easier to leave off the dots and crosses on purpose.

II. What's in a Name?

What You Need:
lined paper and pencil
a watch or clock

What to Do:
1. Draw a line down the center of a sheet of lined paper to make two columns.
2. In one minute, see how many times you can write your full name in the first column. Now use the second column. See how many times you can write your name *backwards* in one minute. (For instance, I would have to write ikuzuS divaD.)

No doubt you will have fewer names in the second column than in the first. Writing your name is a habit—but writing it backwards isn't.

Can you think back to when you first learned to print your name? It used to be hard work for you. Maybe your parents kept some of your first efforts at printing your name. If so, look at them. See how far your brain, nerves, and muscles have taken you since then?

Cerebellum at Work

Take a closer look at just one of the valuable things your cerebellum does for you.

What to Do:

1. Hold your index finger in front of your face, about 15 cm (6 inches) away. Move your hand from side to side, as fast as you can. Does your finger look like a blur?

2. Now hold your finger still, about 15 cm (6 inches) from your face. Turn your head from side to side as fast as you can. Keep your eyes on your finger. Is it less blurry this time?

What's Happening?

Even if your head moves suddenly, your cerebellum makes sure that you can "refix" your eyes on whatever you were looking at. This very handy feature has a long name. It's called (are you ready?) the *vestibulo-ocular reflex*. This reflex can save you from an accident. Suppose that you are riding along on your bicycle. Suddenly you hit a dip in the path. Your whole body bounces up and down. Still, you are able to keep your eyes on a fallen branch lying in your path. You go around it safely.

What's So Funny about a Funny Bone?

The funniest thing about your funny bone is—it isn't a bone at all, it's a nerve! Your elbow is a bony knob with just a thin layer of skin over it. The bony knob is the rounded end of the humerus, the big bone of your upper arm. Running over this knob is the ulnar nerve. When you bang your elbow, you feel a tingling pain in this nerve. You may even feel the pain all the way down into your baby finger, where the ulnar nerve ends. (P.S. If you like puns, you could say this: Although hitting your funny bone isn't funny, it is *humerus*!)

Fantastic Feats of Memory

A man from Burma recited from memory 16,000 pages of Buddhist religious texts in 1974. He had probably studied these texts for a long time, and they made sense, which made them easier to memorize. Nevertheless, this is a huge memory task. Most people couldn't do it.

Another kind of memory feat involves what is called *eidetic* (photographic) memory. Some rare people can replay a picture in their minds of something they saw very briefly. A man in England once memorized the order of cards in six decks (312 cards) shuffled together. He saw them only once. When he recited the cards, he made only 24 mistakes. Do you think that's too many errors? Try memorizing the order of just 20 or 30 playing cards (looking through them once) and see how you do!

The Left-Handed Riddle

There is only one left-handed human being for every nine right-handed ones. Other animals show an even split between those who favor their right paw (or hoof or flipper), and those who lead with their left. Why are human beings different? No one knows.

You might expect left-handers to have left-handed parents. However, most lefties (84 percent) have two right-handed parents. Are their brains a little different? Maybe. Some left-handed people seem to control language with *both* cerebral cortexes, instead of just the left.

In the past, left-handers were sometimes treated as strange beings. Languages show this. Our word *sinister* comes from the Latin word for *left*. The French word *gauche* means both *left* and *awkward*. Of course, left-handed people are no more awkward than anybody else. They just do things the way that feels right (oops, I mean *correct!*) to them.

How You Communicate

*W*hat does *communicating* mean? It means sharing ideas with other people. You tell them something, and they tell you something. There are different ways to communicate. Most people talk to each other. But many people who have trouble talking or hearing use other ways to communicate. They may make signs with their hands. They may point to words or pictures on a board or computer screen. The important thing is that they get their messages across. Every person has thoughts and feelings to communicate.

When you were a baby, you didn't know any words. At first, you used crying to let people know how you felt. Your parents sometimes found your messages hard to understand, though. They knew you were upset about something, but what? They fed you, changed your diaper, or rocked you. If you stopped crying, they hoped they'd solved your problem.

As the months went by, you got better at communicating. When someone smiled at you, you smiled back. You made all kinds of noises—laughs, gurgles, chirps, and spitting sounds. You were also listening carefully to the sounds people made to you. By the time you were around two years old, you were copying these sounds and figuring out when to use them. You were talking!

Where do the sounds come from when you talk? They start in your *larynx*, or voicebox. This is a box-shaped organ that sits at the top of your *trachea*. (The trachea, or windpipe, leads down to your lungs.) The larynx is protected by a knobby piece of cartilage. You can probably see this cartilage. It's the bump in your neck that bobs up and down when you swallow. Some people call it an *Adam's apple*. Men have bigger larynxes than women and children, so their Adam's apples stick out farther.

The larynx is open at both ends, so that air can pass right through. Two strong and stretchy strips lie across the top opening of the larynx. These are your vocal cords. When you are just breathing in and out, your vocal cords are very relaxed. They don't make any noise.

Have you ever played a guitar, banjo, or violin? Perhaps you've watched someone else playing. The strings of these instruments *vibrate* (shake back and forth very fast) when they're plucked. This makes the sound you hear. Vocal cords vibrate, too. When you speak, muscles in your larynx pull the vocal cords tight. Air passing through your throat makes them vibrate. (Do you talk on an in-breath or an out-breath? Try talking both ways and see.)

On a guitar, the thickest string makes the lowest note when it's plucked. Vocal cords work the same way. Men have thicker vocal cords than women, so their voices sound deeper. The more you tighten a guitar string, the higher the note it plays. It's the same with vocal cords. When you sing a high note, you can feel the strain as your vocal cords stretch tighter.

A set of guitar strings attached to a flat board wouldn't make a very loud sound. The hollow body of the guitar is a *resonator* that makes the music louder. You have resonators, too—your chest and the eight hollow spaces in your face called *sinuses*.

Now you know how you make sounds. But how do you make the special different sounds of speech? All the parts of your mouth go into action. How do your lips help you say "baby," "pepper," and "whirlwind"? What do your teeth do when you say "the" and "velvet"? Your tongue taps against the back of your teeth when you say "tickle." What do your teeth and tongue do when you say "sizzle" ? Even your nose is important. Try saying "No plum jam" while pinching your nose. It's hard to say the "n" and the "m's," isn't it?

People who study communication say that words, by themselves, are only a small part of the message. The *way* we say the words–called *tone*-is very important, too. Suppose you say, "How did you do that?" You may want to show you are amazed, angry, happy, or frightened. How can you use your tone so that other people will understand you?

Often you can show your feelings with no words at all. A hug is a communication, and so is a wave. Look in a mirror. Even if you cover the bottom of your face, your eyes can still "smile." (They crinkle at the corners.) They can narrow with anger. They can widen with surprise. *(See page 88)*.

All of these wordless messages are called *body language*. People who study communication say that more than half of what we communicate is shown this way. Smiles and frowns are body language. The way we sit, stand, and walk can also send a message. Someone who is happy may almost skip with joy. Someone who is sad may walk slowly, head down and shoulders hunched.

If you really pay attention to what people are saying—not just with words, but with their faces and bodies—you'll be amazed at how much better you can understand them. You'll become a kinder, wiser person.

Mirror, Mirror, Off the Wall

This is fun and it teaches you to pick up the little signals people give about what they're going to do—*before* they do it.

What You Need:
a friend to work with

What to Do:
1. Stand face to face with your friend. Put the palms of your hands against your friend's palms. Move far enough apart that you can see each other's movements, but close enough so that you can still touch hands easily. Decide who is going to "lead" first. Let's suppose it's you. Now you're both going to pretend that your friend is your reflection in a mirror. Everything you do, your friend has to do, too. Keep those hands together.

2. Start off with simple movements. Bend over to one side. Straighten up. Raise one leg to the side. Lower it. Take astep to the side and do a knee bend, and so on. Which moves work best? Which moves can't you do without "breaking your mirror?"

3. Take turns being the mirror. Maybe you could make up a mirror dance to your favorite record. You'll find that the more you do this, the better you get at anticipating (figuring out ahead of time) what your friend will do next. You might even get so smooth at it that someone watching can't tell who is leading and who is following!

AMAZING FACTS

Speedy Speakers

Very few people can talk faster than 300 words a minute. Some of the fastest speakers are radio and television sports announcers. One British announcer managed to say 176 words in 30 seconds. He was describing a dog race. Just for fun, try counting out loud as fast as you can for 30 seconds. If you say the numbers clearly, you probably can't get past 100.

Hi, How Am I?

If you see a TV news story about trouble in a faraway country, you have no trouble "reading" the sadness or anger in people's faces. Smiles and laughter also mean the same thing all over the world. Here's a game that tests how good you are at reading people's faces.

What You Need:
a friend to work with
20 index cards or small pieces of
   paper
a pencil

What to Do:
1. You're going to make two sets of 10 cards. On the first 10 cards, write these words, one per card: Happiness, Surprise, Fear, Love, Sadness, Disgust, Confusion, Anger, Determination, Boredom.

2. All these words describe emotions (ways of feeling). Do you know what all of them mean? Here are some times when you might be feeling these emotions:

- Happiness. (It's stopped raining! Now we can go on our picnic!)
- Surprise. (Oh, it's you! I thought you weren't coming back for another week!)
- Fear. (I don't have my homework done—again. My teacher will be really mad!)
- Love. (I love Snowflake. She's the best, smartest dog that ever lived!)
- Sadness. (My best friend just moved away.)
- Disgust. (Yuck! There's a worm in my apple.)
- Confusion. (Now, was I supposed to turn left or right when I got to the corner? Maybe I'm walking in the wrong direction—I don't remember seeing that house before.)

- Anger. (How could you do that to me! I thought you were supposed to be my friend!)
- Determination. (I know I left it here. I'm not going home till I find it!)
- Boredom. (I've heard this story a hundred times. If he keeps talking, I may fall asleep.)
  You can probably think of times in your own life when you felt each of these emotions.

3. Now copy the same 10 words onto the other set of cards. Then you take one set of cards, and your friend takes the other. Shuffle the cards, so you don't know what order they're in.

4. You and your friend sit facing each other. Look at a card, without showing it to your friend. Don't say anything. Just think about the emotion and try to show it with your face. Can your friend guess the emotion?

5. Take turns. Which emotions are the easiest to guess? Which are the hardest? Are some emotions easy to mix up with each other?

In real life, mix-ups of emotions can sometimes happen. For instance, a person may just be feeling shy. But you might think he or she is acting unfriendly to you. Being good at reading people's faces is a handy skill. However, sometimes it's best not to decide too quickly what other people are feeling. Take the time to talk to them and find out.

Index